HEBREW
FOR BEGINNERS

FIRST 1000 WORDS

EFFIE DELAROSA

CONTENTS

6-7	TALK
8	NUMBERS
9	FAMILY
10-12	FOOD
13	VEHICLES
14	TRAVEL
15-17	ANIMALS
18-19	TIME
20-23	VERBS
24	SCHOOL

CONTENTS

25-26	JOBS
27	FRUITS
28	VEGETABLES
29	FEELINGS
30-32	ADJECTIVES
33	NATURE
34	CULTURE
35	COLORS
36	SHAPES & DIRECTIONS
37-40	HOME

CONTENTS

41	PREPOSITIONS
42-44	HUMAN
45	TIME (2)
46-49	COUNTRIES
50	CLOTHES
51	ACCESSORIES
52	SPACE
53	SHOPPING
54-56	ADVERBS
57	PEOPLE

58	SPORT
59	WORLD
60-61	INTERNET
62-63	VOCABULARY
64	TOOLS
65-66	HEALTH-SCIENCE
67	CITY
68	MATERIALS
69	EARTH
70	MUSIC
71	MAIL
72	ECOLOGY

כן
Ken

Yes

לא
Lo

No

שלום
Shalom

Hello

תודה
Toda

Thank You

להתראות
Lehitra'ot

Goodbye

בבקשה
Bevakasha

Please

-ו
Ve
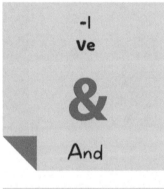
And

או
O

Or

זה
Ze

This

אני
Ani

I

אתה
Ata

You

הוא
Hu
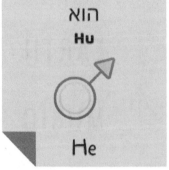
He

היא
Hee

She

אנחנו
Anachnu

We

הם
Hem

They

סליחה	אבל	ערב טוב
Slicha	**Aval**	**Erev tov**
Sorry	But	Good evening

כי	ברוכים הבאים	איפה
Kee	**Bruchim Habaim**	**Eifo**
Because	Welcome	Where

מה	כמה	איזה
Ma	**Kama**	**Eize**
What	How much	Which

מדהים	חמוד	עזרה
Madhim	**Hamud**	**Ezra**
Awesome	Cute	Help

אם	כאשר	למה
Im	**Ka'asher**	**Lama**
If	When	Why

מספרים

MISPARIM

NUMBERS

אפס **0** **Efes** Zero	אחת **1** **Achat** One	שתיים **2** **Shtayim** Two
שלוש **3** **Shalosh** Three	ארבע **4** **Arba** Four	חמש **5** **Chamesh** Five
שש **6** **Shes** Six	שבע **7** **Sheva** Seven	שמונה **8** **Shmone** Eight
תשע **9** **Tesha** Nine	עשר **10** **Eser** Ten	חמשעשרה **15** **Hameshesre** Fifteen
עשרים **20** **Esrim** Twenty	מאה **100** **Elef** One Hundred	עשרת אלפים **1000** **Aseret alafim** One Thousand

משפחה
MISHPACHA

FAMILY

אמא
Ima
Mother

אבא
Aba
Father

אח
Ach
Brother

אחות
Achot
Sister

סבתא
Savta
Grandmother

סבא
Saba
Grandfather

בן
Ben
Son

בת
Bat
Daughter

דודה
Doda
Aunt

דוד
Dod
Uncle

נכדה
Nechda
Granddaughter

נכד
Neched
Grandson

אישה
Isha
Wife

בעל
Ba'al
Husband

ארוחת בוקר
Aruchat boker
Breakfast

ארוחת צהריים
Aruchat tzohoraim
Lunch

לחם
Lechem
Bread

ארוחת ערב
Aruchat erev
Dinner

ארוחה
Arucha
Meal

גבינה
Gvina
Cheese

ביצה
Beitza
Egg

דג
Dag
Fish

בשר
Basar
Meat

חמאה
Chem'aa
Butter

נקניקיה
Naknikiyah
Sausage

יוגורט
Yogurt
Yogurt

עוגה
Uga
Cake

שוקולד
Shokolad
Chocolate

מלח
Melach
Salt

סוכר
Sukar
Sugar

קמח
Kemach
Flour

פלפל
Pilpel
Pepper

משקה
Mashke
Drink

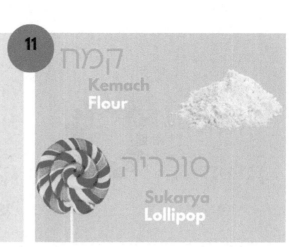

סוכריה
Sukarya
Lollipop

דבש
Dvash
Honey

סופגניה
Sufganiyah
Doughnut

גלידה
Glida
Ice Cream

מים
Mayim
Water

קפה
Cafe
Coffee

חלב
Chalav
Milk

מיץ תפוזים
Mitz tapuzim
Orange Juice

תה
Te
Tea

שוקו
Shoko
Hot Chocolate

אוכל
Ochel
Food

ויטמין
Vitamin
Vitamin

בצל
Batzal
Onion

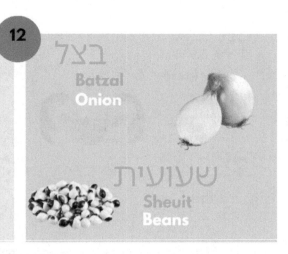

קינוח
Kinuach
Dessert

דגני בוקר
Digney boker
Cereals

שעועית
Sheuit
Beans

תירס
Tiras
Corn

חיטה
Chita
Wheat

שיבול שועל
Shibolet shual
Oat

קטשופ
Ketshop
Ketchup

חרדל
Chardal
Mustard

תבלינים
Tavlinim
Spices

שמן
Shemen
Oil

אורז
Orez
Rice

פסטה
Pasta
Pasta

רכבים
rechavim

vehicles

מטוס
MATOS

AIRPLANE

סירה
SIRA

BOAT

ספינה
SFINA

SHIP

אוטו
OTO

CAR

אופנוע
OFNOA

MOTORBIKE

רכבת
RAKEVET

TRAIN

טרקטור
TRACTOR

TRACTOR

אופניים
OFANAIM

BICYCLE

אוטובוס
OTOBUS

BUS

מונית
MONIT

TAXI

רכבת תחתית
RAKEVET TACHTIT

SUBWAY

משאית
MASA'IT

TRUCK

אמבולנס
AMBULANCE

AMBULANCE

מסוק
MASOK

HELICOPTER

רכבת חשמלית
RAKEVET CHASHMALIT

TRAM

חופשה	שדה תעופה	תחנת רכבת
HUFSHA	**SDE TEUFA**	**TCHANAT RAKEVET**
HOLIDAY	AIRPORT	TRAIN STATION

נמל	תייר	בית מלון
NAMAL	**TAYAR**	**BEIT MALON**
PORT	TOURIST	HOTEL

בית	דירה	מזוודה
BAIT	**DIRA**	**MIZVADA**
HOUSE	APARTMENT	SUITCASE

דרכון	מפה	בריכה
DARKON	**MAPA**	**BREICHA**
PASSPORT	MAP	SWIMMING POOL

דרך	רחוב	הליכה
DERECH	**RECHOV**	**HALICHA**
ROAD	STREET	WALK

ציפור
Tzipor

Bird

חתול
Chatul

Cat

כלב
Kelev

Dog

ברווז
Barvaz

Duck

עכבר
Achbar

Mouse

יונה
Yona

Pigeon

ארנב
Arnav

Rabbit

פיל
Pil

Elephant

קוף
Kof

Monkey

CHAYOT

תרנגול
Tarnegol

Chicken

פרה
Para

Cow

חמור
Chamor

Donkey

עז
Ez

Goat

סוס
Sus

Horse

חזיר
Chazir

Pig

ANIMALS

כבשה
Kivsa

Sheep

אווז
Avaz

Goose

דב
Dov

Bear

גמל
Gamal

Camel

צפרדע
Tzfarde'a

Frog

נחש
Nachash

Snake

צב
Tzav

Turtle

זאב
Ze'ev

Wolf

תנין
Tanin

Crocodile

דינוזאור
Dinozaur

Dinosaur

ג'ירפה
Jirafa

Giraffe

קנגורו
Kenguru

Kangaroo

לטאה
Leta'a

Lizard

נמר
Namer

Tiger

זברה
Zebra

Zebra

חיות

CHAYOT

ANIMALS

כריש **Karish**  Shark	סרטן **Sartan**  Crab	דולפין **Dolphin**  Dolphin
מדוזה **Meduza**  Jellyfish	לובסטר **Lobster**  Lobster	סוסון ים **Suson yam**  Seahorse
חתול ים **Chatul yam**  Ray	תמנון **Tamnun**  Octopus	פרפר **Parpar**  Butterfly
ג'וק **Juk**  Cockroach	עכביש **Akavish**  Spider	חיפושית **Chipushit**  Beetle
שפירית **Shapirit**  Dragonfly	נמלה **Nemala**  Ant	דבורה **Dvora**  Bee

יום YOM			DAY
שני SHENI MONDAY	שלישי SHLISHI TUESDAY	רביעי REVI'I WEDNESDAY	חמישי CHAMISHI THURSDAY
שישי SHISHI FRIDAY	שבת SHABBAT SATURDAY	ראשון RISHON SUNDAY	שבוע SHAVUA WEEK

זמן ZMAN		TIME
שעה SHA'A HOUR	דקה DAKA MINUTE	

18

שנה SHANA	YEAR

חודש CHODESH	MONTH

ינואר YANUAR JANUARY	פברואר FEBRUAR FEBRUARY	מרץ MERTZ MARCH	אפריל APRIL APRIL
מאי MAY MAY	יוני YUNI JUNE	יולי YULI JULY	אוגוסט OGUST AUGUST
ספטמבר SEPTEMBER SEPTEMBER	אוקטובר OCTOBER OCTOBER	נובמבר NOVEMBER NOVEMBER	דצמבר DETZEMBER DECEMBER

חורף
Choref
Winter

אביב
Aviv
Spring

עונה
Ona
Season

סתיו
Stav
Autumn

קיץ
Kaitz
Summer

רוח
Ruach
Wind

גשם
Geshem
Rain

סופת רעמים
Sufat re'amim
Thunderstorm

בוקר
Boker
Morning

אחר הצהריים
Achar tzohorayim
Afternoon

לילה
Layla
Night

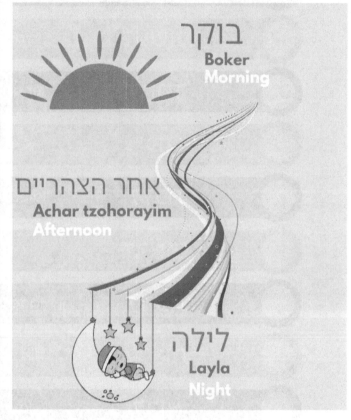

אקלים
Aklim
Climate

הווה
Hove
Present

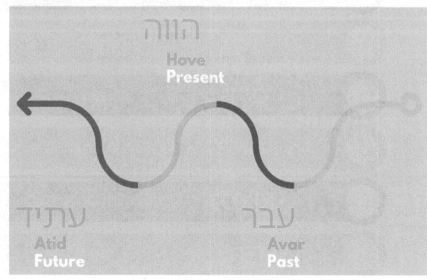

עתיד
Atid
Future

עבר
Avar
Past

יש	yesh	have
להיות	lehiyot	be
לעשות	la'asot	do
להגיד	lehagid	say
יכול	ychol	can
ללכת	lalechet	go
לראות	lir'ot	see
לדעת	lada'at	know
לרצות	lirtzot	want
לבוא	lavo	come
צריך	tzarich	need
חייב	chayav	have to
להאמין	leha'amin	believe
למצוא	limtzo	find
לתת	latet	give

פעלים

PE'ALIM

VERBS

לקחת	lakachat	take
לדבר	ledaber	talk
לשים	lasim	put
נדמה	nidme	seem
לעזוב	la'azov	leave
להישאר	lehisha'er	stay
לחשוב	lachshov	think
להסתכל	lehistakel	look
לענות	la'anot	answer
לחכות	lechakot	wait
לחיות	lichyot	live
להבין	lehavin	understand
להיכנס	lehikanes	come in
להפוך	lahafoch	become
לחזור	lachzor	come back

פעלים
PE'ALIM

VERBS

לכתוב	lichtov	write
להתקשר	lehitkasher	call
ליפול	lipol	fall
להתחיל	lehatchil	start
לעקוב	la'akov	follow
להראות	lehar'ot	show
לצחוק	litzchok	laugh
לחייך	lechayech	smile
לזכור	lizkor	remember
לשחק	lesachek	play
לאכול	le'echol	eat
לקרוא	likro	read
לקבל	lekabel	get
לבכות	livkot	cry
להסביר	lehasbir	explain

לשיר	lashir	sing
לגעת	laga'at	touch
להריח	lehari'ach	smell
לנשום	linshom	breathe
לשמוע	lishmo'a	hear
לצבוע	litzbo'a	paint
ללמוד	lilmod	study
לחגוג	lachgog	celebrate
לבחור	livchor	choose
לחפש	lechapes	search
לשאול	lish'ol	ask
ליהנות	lehanot	enjoy
לדמיין	ledamyen	imagine
לשתות	lishtot	drink
לשנות	leshanot	change

אלף בית
Alef Bet
Alphabet

עיפרון
Iparon
Pencil

מספריים
Misparayim
Scissors

מחברת
Machberet
Notebook

ילקוט
Yalkut
Schoolbag

תלמיד
Talmid
Student

כיתה
Kita
Classroom

חברים
Chaverim
Friends

פרופסור
Professor
Professor

מתמטיקה
Matematika
Mathematics

$$1+3=$$
$$2\times2=$$

היסטוריה
Historiyah
History

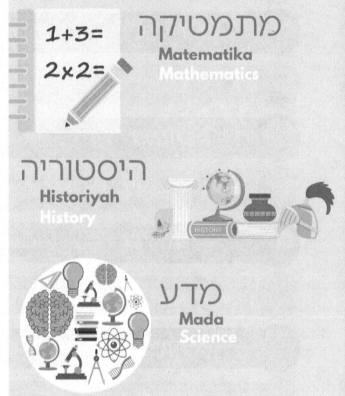

מדע
Mada
Science

בית-ספר
Beit-sefer
School

אומנות
Omanut
Arts

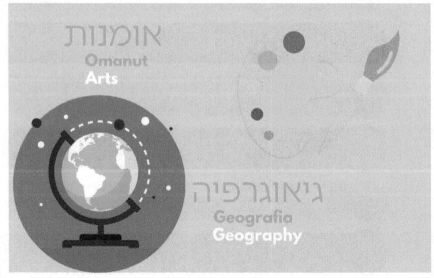

גיאוגרפיה
Geografia
Geography

עבודה
avoda

job

אח
ACH

NURSE

חקלאי
CHAKLAY

FARMER

אדריכל
ADRICHAL

ARCHITECT

מהנדס
MEHANDES

ENGINEER

פועל
PO'EL

LABORER

לוחם אש
LOHEM ESH

FIREFIGHTER

גבן
GANAN

GARDENER

עורך דין
ORECH DIN

LAWYER

טייס
TAYAS

PILOT

שחקן
SACHKAN

ACTOR

שיננית
SHINANIT

DENTIST

מכונאי
MECHONNA'I

MECHANIC

פועל ניקיון
PO'EL NIKAYON

DUSTMAN

רואה חשבון
RO'E CHESHBON

ACCOUNTANT

פסיכולוג
PSICHOLOG

PSYCHOLOGIST

עבודה
avoda

job

עיתונאי
ITONAY
JOURNALIST

נגר
NAGAR
CARPENTER

מוזיקאי
MUSICAY
MUSICIAN

אינסטלטור
INSTELATOR
PLUMBER

טבח
TABACH
COOK

סופר
SOFER
WRITER

ספר
SAPAR
HAIRDRESSER

מזכיר
MAZKIR
SECRETARY

נהג
NAHAG
DRIVER

שוטר
SHOTER
POLICEMAN

רופא
ROFE
DOCTOR

וטרינר
VETRINAR
VETERINARIAN

אופטיקאי
OPTIKAY
OPTICIAN

רופא ילדים
ROFE YELADIM
PEDIATRICIAN

מלצר
MELTZAR
WAITER

שזיף
Shezif
PLUM

אפרסק
Afarsek
PEACH

דובדבן
Duvdevan
CHERRY

תפוח
Tapuach
APPLE

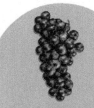

ענבים
Anavim
GRAPE

אבטיח
Avatiach
WATERMELON

אננס
Ananas
PINEAPPLE

תות
Tut
STRAWBERRY

פטל
Petel
RASPBERRY

אגס
Agas
PEAR

בננה
Banana
BANANA

מלון
Melon
MELON

לימון
Limon
LEMON

פטל שחור
Petel shahor
BLACKBERRY

תפוז
Tapuz
ORANGE

פטריה
Pitriyah
MUSHROOM

ברוקולי
Brokoli
BROCCOLI

כרוב
Kruv
CABBAGE

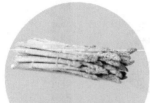

אספרגוס
Asparagus
ASPARAGUS

מלפפון
Melafefon
CUCUMBER

גזר
Gezer
CARROT

צנון
Tznon
RADISH

חסה
Chasa
LETTUCE

תפוח אדמה
Tapu'ach adama
POTATO

עגבניה
Agvaniyah
TOMATO

אבוקדו
Avokado
AVOCADO

כרישה
Krisha
LEEK

סלק
Selek
BEETROOT

חציל
Chatzil
EGGPLANT

ארטישוק
Artishok
ARTICHOKE

רגוע
Ragua
Calm

שמח
Same'ach
Happy

מאוכזב
Me'uchzav
Disappointed

נרגש
Nirgash
Excited

מבוהל
Mevohal
Frightened

מרוגז
Merugaz
Grumpy

מאוהב
Me'ohav
In Love

מופתע
Mufta
Surprised

מתבייש
Mitbayesh
Shy

29

גאה
Ge'e
Proud

כועס
Ko'es
Angry

מבולבל
Mevulbal
Confused

עייף
Ayef
Tired

לחוץ
Lachutz
Nervous

סקרן
Sakran
Curious

שמות תואר
smot to'ar

adjectives

פנטסטי	fantasti	fantastic
משונה	meshune	weird
קשה	kashe	hard
מצחיק	matzchik	funny
מוזר	muzar	strange
קל	kal	easy
בלתי אפשרי	bilti efshari	impossible
צעיר	tza'ir	young
נכון	nachon	correct
חופשי	chofshi	free
חולה	chole	sick
אותו דבר	oto davar	same
עני	ani	poor
אפשרי	efshari	possible
נקי	naki	clean

שמות תואר
smot to'ar

adjectives

מלוכלך	meluchlach	dirty
פשוט	pashut	simple
עצוב	atzuv	sad
ריק	rek	empty
טוב	tov	good
רך	rach	soft
שקרי	shikri	false
גדול	gadol	big
רע	ra	bad
רציני	retzini	serious
ישן	yashan	old
אמיתי	amiti	true
יפה	yafe	beautiful
חם	cham	hot
קר	kar	cold

שמות תואר
smot to'ar

adjectives

יקר	yakar	expensive
נקי	naki	clear
אחרון	acharon	last
שונה	shone	different
חזק	chazak	strong
נחמד	nechmad	nice
גבוה	gavoha	high
אנושי	enoshi	human
חשוב	chashuv	important
יפה	yafe	pretty
קל	kal	light
קטן	katan	small
חדש	chadash	new
מלא	ma'le	full
ראשון	rishon	first

דשא
Deshe
Grass

חרק
Chrek
Insect

פרח
Perach
Flower

אוויר
Avir
Air

שלג
Sheleg
Snow

הר
Har
Mountain

ענן
Anan
Cloud

שמיים
Shamayim
Sky

ערפל
Arafel
Fog

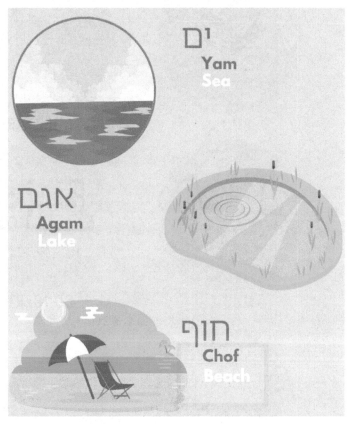

ים
Yam
Sea

אגם
Agam
Lake

חוף
Chof
Beach

שמש
Shemesh
Sun

יער
Ya'ar
Forest

עץ
Etz
Tree

עיתון
Iton
NEWSPAPER

קולנוע
Kolno'a
CINEMA

טלוויזיה
Televizya
TELEVISION

ספר
Sefer
BOOK

פיסול
Pisul
SCULPTURE

צילום
Tzilum
PHOTOGRAPHY

מוזיקה
Musika
MUSIC

קונצרט
Konzert
CONCERT

סרט
Seret
MOVIE

מחשב
Machshev
COMPUTER

מילון
Milon
DICTIONARY

ציור
Tziur
PAINTING

מוזיאון
Moze'on
MUSEUM

אופרה
Opera
OPERA

תיאטרון
Te'atron
THEATER

צבעים
TZVA'IM

COLORS

כחול	kachol	blue
סגול	sagol	purple
ורוד	varod	pink
אדום	adom	red
כתום	katom	orange
צהוב	tzahov	yellow
ירוק	yarok	green

שחור	shachor	black
לבן	lavan	white
חום	chum	brown
זהב	zahav	gold
אפור	afor	gray
כסף	kesef	silver
קשת	keshet	rainbow

מלפני	milfaney	in front of
מאחורי	me'achorey	behind
שמאל	smol	left
ימין	yemin	right
אמצע	emtza	middle
ריבוע	ribu'a	square
עיגול	igul	circle
מלבן	malben	rectangle
קוביה	kubia	cube
יהלום	yahalom	diamond
שורה	shura	line
מערב	ma'arav	west
מזרח	mizrach	east
צפון	tzafon	north
דרום	darom	south

מטבח	דלת	פינת אוכל	שירותים
MITBACH	DELET	PINAT OCHEL	SHERUTIM
KITCHEN	DOOR	DINING ROOM	BATHROOM

חלון	מדרגות	עליית גג	מסדרון
CHALON	MADREGOT	ALIYAT GAG	MISDARON
WINDOW	STAIRS	ATTIC	HALL

משרד	מרפסת	מרתף	שכן
MISRAD	MIRPESET	MARTEF	SHACHEN
OFFICE	BALCONY	BASEMENT	NEIGHBOR

גינה	חדר שינה
GINA	CHADAR SHEYNA
GARDEN	BEDROOM

תנור	רדיאטור	ספה	מקרר
TANUR	RADIATOR	SAPA	MEKARER
OVEN	RADIATOR	SOFA	FRIDGE

 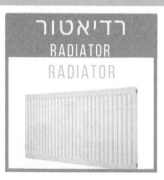  

מנורה	כיור	טלפון	כוס
MENORA	KIOR	TELEFON	KOS
LAMP	SINK	TELEPHONE	GLASS

צלחת	מראה	שעון	כיסא
TZALACHAT	MAR'AA	SHA'ON	KISE
PLATE	MIRROR	CLOCK	CHAIR

מיטה	שולחן
MITA	SHULCHAN
BED	TABLE

קיר	גג	מקפיא	ארון
KIR	GAG	MAKPI	ARON
WALL	ROOF	FREEZER	CUPBOARD

צמח	אח	שואב אבק	ברז
TZEMACH	ACH	SOEV AVAK	BEREZ
PLANT	FIREPLACE	VACUUM CLEANER	TAP

מדיח	מיקרוגל	שטיח	פעמון
MEDIACH	MIKROGAL	SHATIACH	PA'AMON
DISHWASHER	MICROWAVE	CARPET	DOORBELL

תריס	מפתח
TRIS	MAFTEACH
SHUTTER	KEY

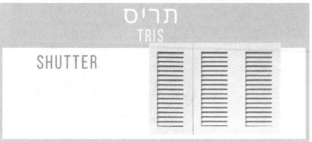 

מגבת
MAGEVET
TOWEL

מצעים
MATZA'IM
BED SHEET

סבון
SABON
SOAP

מסרק
MASREK
COMB

וילון
VILON
CURTAIN

ספל
SEFEL
CUP

מקלחת
MIKLACHAT
SHOWER

נורה
NURA
LIGHTBULB

מזלג
MAZLEG
FORK

כף
KAF
SPOON

סכין
SAKIN
KNIFE

אמבטיה
AMBATYA
BATHTUB

בקבוק
BAKBUK
BOTTLE

פח זבל
PACH ZEVEL
GARBAGE CAN

בשביל	bishvil	for
אחרי	achrey	after
לפני	lifney	before
עם	im	with
לגבי	legabey	about
נגד	neged	against
בתוך	betoch	in
בלי	bli	without
מאז	me'az	since
מסביב	misaviv	around
על	al	on
כמו	kmo	like
במשך	bemeshech	during
בין	bein	between
-מ	me	from

גוף guf body	ראש rosh head 	יד yad hand
שיער se'ar hair 	פנים panim face 	אצבע etzba finger 
אוזן ozen ear 	עיניים eynayim eyes	ציפורן tziporen nail
אף af nose 	פה pe mouth	רגל regel leg 
שן shen tooth	שפתיים sfatayim lips	כף רגל kaf regel foot

גוף האדם
Guf ha'adam

Human

מוח
moach

brain

דם
sam

blood

לב
lev

heart

קיבה
keyva

stomach

כבד
kaved

liver

כליה
kiliya

kidney

ריאות
re'ot

lungs

מעיים
me'ayim

intestine

טבור
tabur

navel

כתף
katef

shoulder

לשון
lashon

tongue

בטן
beten

belly

ירך
yarech

hip

ברך
berech
knee

עקב
akev

ankle

עור or skin 	עצם etzem bone 	גולגולת gulgolet skull 
צוואר tzavar neck 	מפרק כף היד mifrak kaf hayad wrist 	גבה gaba eyebrow 
גרון garon throat 	עפעף afaf eyelid 	סנטר santer chin
זקן zakan beard 	שפם safam mustache 	שריר shrir muscle 
מרפק marpek elbow	בוהן bohen toe 	לחי lechi cheek 

זמן
zman

time

אתמול	etmol	yesterday
היום	hayom	today
מחר	machar	tomorrow
עכשיו	achshav	now
בקרוב	bekarov	soon
מאוחר	me'uchar	late
כאן	kan	here
מרחק	merchak	distance
זריחה	zricha	sunrise
צהריים	tzaharayim	noon
ערב	erev	evening
חצות	chatzot	midnight
עשור	asor	decade
מאה	me'a	century
אלף שנה	elef shana	millennium

אירופה
Eropa

Europe

אפריקה
Afrika

Africa

אסיה
Asya

Asia

אמריקה
Amerika

America

אנגליה
Angliya

England

גרמניה
Germanya

Germany

צרפת
Tzarfat

France

ספרד
Sfarad

Spain

איטליה
Italya

Italy

ארצות הברית
Arzot Habrit

United States

ברזיל
Brazil

Brazil

יפן
Yapan

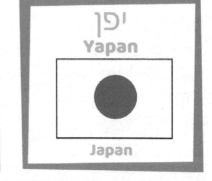

Japan

סין
Sin

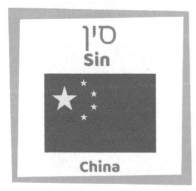

China

הודו
Hodu

India

רוסיה
Rusya

Russia

מדינה

MEDINA

COUNTRY

מקסיקו
Mexico

Mexico

מצרים
Mitzrayim

Egypt

תורכיה
Turkya

Turkey

ניגריה
Nigeria

Nigeria

תאילנד
Tailand

Thailand

דרום קוריאה
Drom kore'a

South Korea

קולומביה
Kolombia

Colombia

ארגנטינה
Argentina

Argentina

אלג'יריה
Aljiriya

Algeria

פולין
Polin

Poland

ערב הסעודית
Arav hasa'udit

Saudi Arabia

קמרון
Kameron

Cameroon

הולנד
Holand

Netherlands

שווייץ
Shvaitz

Switzerland

שבדיה
Shvedia

Sweden

מדינה

MEDINA

COUNTRY

יוון
Yavan

Greece

בלגיה
Belgia

Belgium

אירלנד
Irland

Ireland

נורווגיה
Norvegia

Norway

אוסטרליה
Ostralia

Australia

דנמרק
Denmark

Denmark

אוסטריה
Ostria

Austria

פינלנד
Finland

Finland

פורטוגל
Portugal

Portugal

דרום אפריקה
Drom afrika

South Africa

אינדונזיה
Indonezia

Indonesia

טנזניה
Tanzania

Tanzania

אוקראינה
Ukrayna

Ukraine

פרו
Peru

Peru

צ'ילה
Chille

Chile

מדינה

MEDINA

COUNTRY

אירופאי
Erope'i

European

אמריקאי
Amerika'i

American

אנגלי
Angli

English

צרפתי
Tzarfati

French

ספרדי
Sfaradi

Spanish

איטלקי
Italki

Italien

גרמני
Germani

German

אפריקאי
Afrika'i

African

אסייתי
Asiati

Asian

רוסי
Rusi

Russian

סיני
Sini

Chinese

קנדי
Kanadi

Canadien

הודי
Hodi

Indian

ברזילאי
Brazila'i

Brazilian

מקסיקני
Mexikani

Mexican

אוכלוסיה

UCHLUSIA

POPULATION

מכנסיים חצאית
Michnasayim **Chatza'it**
Pants **Shirt**

עניבה גרביים
Aniva **Garbayim**
Tie **Socks**

ז'קט
Jaket
Jacket

משקפיים
Mishkafayim
Glasses

חגורה
Chagora
Belt

כובע
Kova
Hat

נעליים שמלה
Na'alayim **Simla**
Shoes **Dress**

ארנק
Arnak
Wallet

מטריה
Mitriya
Umbrella

כובע צמר צעיף
Kova tzemer **Tze'if**
Beanie **Scarf**

כפפות
Kfafot
Gloves

אביזרים
avizarim

accessories

צמיד
TZAMID
BRACELET

שעון
SHA'ON
WATCH

תכשיט
TACHSHIT
JEWELRY

טבעת
TABA'AT
RING

עגילים
AGILIM
EARRINGS

ממחטה
MIMCHATA
HANDKERCHIEF

פיג'מה
PIJAMA
PAJAMAS

סנדלים
SANDALIM
SANDALS

מגפיים
MAGAFAYIM
BOOTS

שרוך
SROCH
SHOELACE

שרשרת
SHARSHERET
NECKLACE

נעלי בית
NA'ALEY BAIT
SLIPPERS

איפור
IPUR
MAKEUP

תיק צד
TIK TZAD
HANDBAG

כיס
KIS
POCKET

יקום
Yekum
Universe

גלקסיה
Glaxya
Galaxy

כוכב שביט
Kochav shavit
Comet

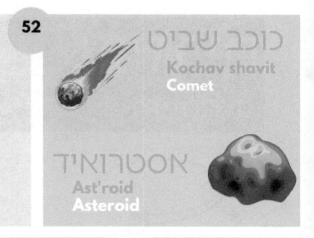

שביל החלב
Shvil hachalav
Milky Way

חלל
Chalal
Space

אסטרואיד
Ast'roid
Asteroid

ירח
Yare'ach
Moon

כדור הארץ
Kadur ha'aretz
Earth

כוכב
Kochav
Star

זמן
Zman
Time

אור
Or
Light

כוכב לכת
Kochav lechet
Planet

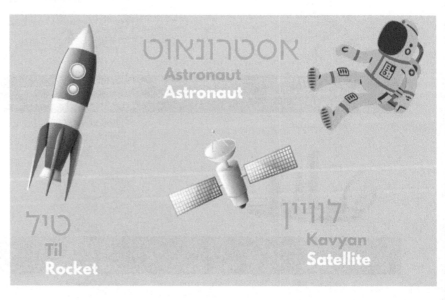

אסטרונאוט
Astronaut
Astronaut

טיל
Til
Rocket

לוויין
Kavyan
Satellite

מחיר
Mechir
Price

כסף
Kesef
Money

מתנה
Matana
Gift

לשלם
Keshalem
To pay

לקוח
Lko'ach
Client

אונליין
Online
Online

בית מרקחת
Ceit mirkachat
Pharmacy

בנק
Bank
Bank

חנות
Chanut
Store

חנות ספרים
Sfarim
Bookstore

מסעדה
Mis'aada
Restaurant

מסיבה
Mesiba
Party

חתונה
Chatuna
Wedding

לידה
Leyda
Birth

יום הולדת
Yom huledet
Birthday

תואר הפועל
to'ar hapo'al

adverbs

תמיד	tamid	always
במקום אחר	bmakom acher	elsewhere
בערך	be'erech	approximately
בכל מקום	bechol makom	everywhere
איפשהו	eyfoshehu	somewhere
בכל מקום	bechol makom	anywhere
בשום מקום	beshum makom	nowhere
בפנים	bifnim	inside
בחוץ	bachutz	outside
לכן	lachen	thus
קרוב	karov	near
מעל	me'al	above
באיטיות	be'itiut	slowly
במהירות	bimhirut	quickly
באמת	be'emet	really

תואר הפועל
to'ar hapo'al

adverbs

בפשטות	bepashtut	simply
ברצינות	birtzinut	seriously
למרבה המזל	lrmarbe hamazal	fortunately
לפעמים	lif'amim	sometimes
לעתים רחוקות	le'itim rechokot	rarely
מספיק	maspik	enough
קודם כל	kodem kol	firstly
לפני	lifney	before
אחרי	acharey	after
למרות	lamrot	however
אף פעם	af pa'am	never
לאחרונה	la'achrona	recently
אז	az	then
לעתים קרובות	le'itim krovot	often
בדרך כלל	bederech klal	usually

תואר הפועל
to'ar hapo'al

adverbs

טוב יותר	tov yoter	better
היטב	heytev	well
הרבה	harbe	a lot
מעדיף	ma'adif	rather
די	dey	quite
אז	az	so
גם	gam	too
קצת	ktzat	little
רחוק	rachok	far
מאוד	me'od	very
כמעט	kim'at	almost
כבר	kvar	already
מאז	me'az	since
לפתע	lefeta	suddenly
אכן	achen	indeed

תינוק
Tinok
Baby

ילד
Yeled
Child

בן
Brn
Boy

בת
Bat
Girl

מתבגר
Mitbager
Teenager

אישה
Isha
Woman

גבר
Gever
Man

מבוגר
Mevugar
Adult

חבר
Chaver
Friend

אחיין
Achyan
Cousin

עמית
Amit
Colleague

אהבה
Ahava
Love

חברות
Chaverut
Friendship

שמחה
Simcha
Happiness

אושר
Osher
Joy

אנשים

anashim

people

57

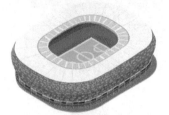

צוות	שחקן	אצטדיון
TZEVET	**SCHKAN**	**ITZTADYON**
TEAM	PLAYER	STADIUM

כדורגל	שופט	כדור
KADUREGEL	**SHOFET**	**KDUR**
FOOTBALL/SOCCER	REFEREE	BALL

חולצה	אימון	דירוג
CHULTZA	**IMUN**	**DIRUG**
JERSEY	TRAINING	RANKING

רכיבת סוסים	רכיבה	שחייה
RECHIVAT SUSIM	**RECHIVA**	**SCHIYA**
HORSE RIDING	CYCLING	SWIMMING

מאמן	פציעה	מסלול
ME'AMEN	**PTZI'A**	**MASLUL**
COACH	INJURY	TRACK AND FIELD

ממשלה
Memshala
Government

נשיא
Nasi
President

פוליטיקאים
Politicayim
Politics

ראש ממשלה
Rosh memshala
Mayor

עולם
Olam
World

מדינה
Medina
Country

אנשים
Anashim
People

יבשת
Yabeshet
Continent

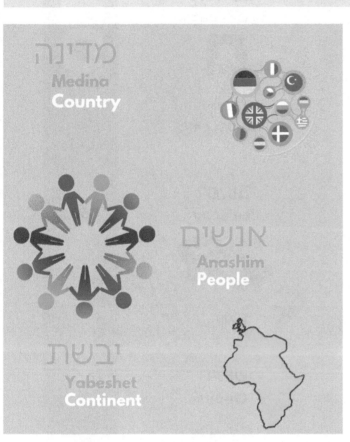

עיר
It
City

ישוב
Yeshuv
Town

פארק
Park
Park

חברה
Chevra
Company

אי
Ee
Island

מדבר
Midbar
Desert

בית חולים
Beit Cholim
Hospital

מדיה חברתית
Medya chevratit

Social network

משתמש
Mishtames

User

לפרסם
Lefarsem

Publish

לשתף
Leshatef

Share

תוכן
Tochen

Content

להירשם
Lehirashem

Subscribe

חדשות
Chadashot

News

פרסום
Pirsum

Advertising

לעקוב
La'acov

Follow

חשבון
Cheshbon

Account

ערוץ
Arutz

Channel

חיפוש
Chipus

Research

תגובה
Tguva

Comment

צ'אט
Chet

Chat

קישור
Kishur

Link

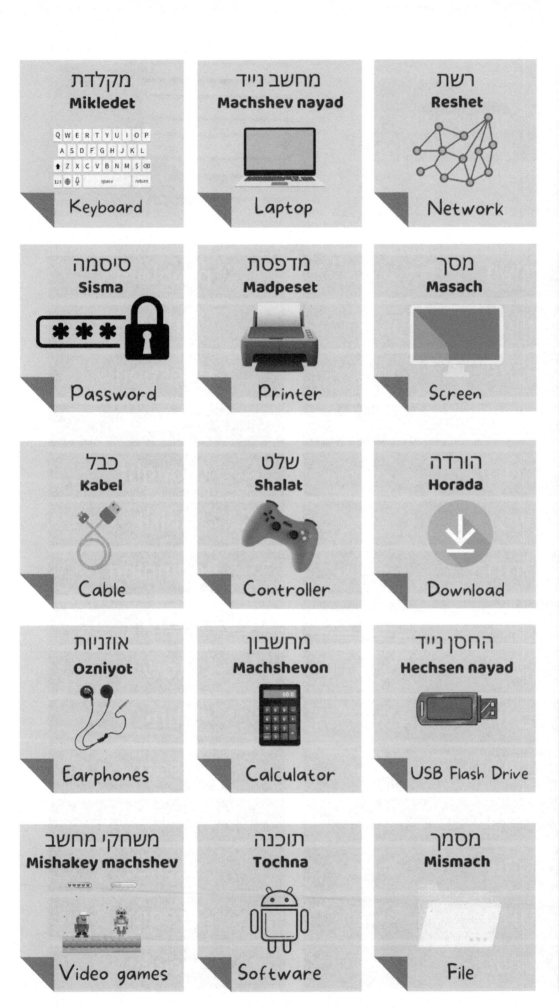

מקלדת **Mikledet** Keyboard	מחשב נייד **Machshev nayad** Laptop	רשת **Reshet** Network
סיסמה **Sisma** Password	מדפסת **Madpeset** Printer	מסך **Masach** Screen
כבל **Kabel** Cable	שלט **Shalat** Controller	הורדה **Horada** Download
אוזניות **Ozniyot** Earphones	מחשבון **Machshevon** Calculator	החסן נייד **Hechsen nayad** USB Flash Drive
משחקי מחשב **Mishakey machshev** Video games	תוכנה **Tochna** Software	מסמך **Mismach** File

בעיה	beáya	problem
רעיון	raáyon	idea
שאלה	sheéla	question
תשובה	tshuva	answer
מחשבה	machshava	thought
נפש	nefesh	spirit
התחלה	hatchala	beginning
סוף	sof	end
חוק	chok	law
חיים	cayim	life
מוות	mavet	death
שלום	shalom	peace
שקט	sheket	silence
חלום	chalom	dream
משקל	mishkal	weight

דיעה	deá	opinion
דבר	davar	thing
טעות	taút	mistake
רעב	raáv	hunger
צמא	tzama	thirst
בחירה	bchira	choice
כוח	koách	strength
תמונה	tmuna	picture
רובוט	robot	robot
שקר	sheker	lie
אמת	emet	truth
רעש	raásh	noise
כלום	klum	nothing
הכל	hakol	everything
חצי	chetzi	half

גרזן
GARZEN
AXE

מקדחה
MAKDECHA
DRILL

דבק
DEVEK
GLUE

פטיש
PATISH
HAMMER

סולם
SULAM
LADDER

מסמר
MASMER
NAIL

מברג
MAVREG
SCREWDRIVER

מגרפה
MAGREFA
RAKE

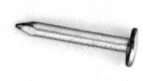

מכסחת דשא
MEKASACHAT DESHE
MOWER

מסור
MASOR
SAW

קרטון
KARTON
CARDBOARD

מריצה
MERITZA
WHEELBARROW

משפך
MASHPECH
WATERING CAN

בורג
BOREG
SCREW

את
ET
SHOVEL

אוצר מילים
otzar milim

vocabulary

אלרגיה	alergia	allergy
שפעת	shapa't	flu
מנוחה	menucha	rest
תרופה	trufa	medication
חיסון	chisun	vaccine
אנטיביוטיקה	antibyotika	antibiotic
חום	chom	fever
ריפוי	ripuy	heal
בריאות	bri'ut	health
זיהום	zihum	infection
תסמין	tasmin	symptom
מדבק	medabek	contagious
חולי	choli	sickness
כאב	ke'ev	pain
שיעול	shi'ul	cough

אטום
Atom

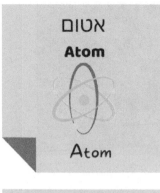

Atom

בקטריה
Bakterya

Bacterium

תא
Ta

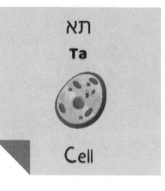

Cell

כימיה
Chimia

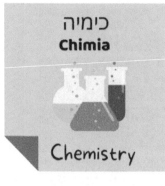

Chemistry

ביולוגיה
Biyologya

Biology

מיקרוסקופ
Mikroskop

Microscope

מולקולה
Molekula

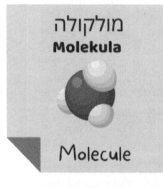

Molecule

חישוב
Chishuv

Calculation

תוצאה
Totza'a

Result

חיבור
Chibur

Addition

חיסור
Chisur

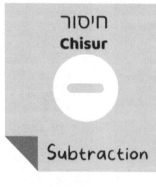

Subtraction

חילוק
Chishuv

Division

כפל
Kefel

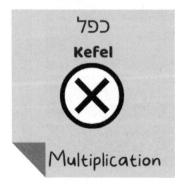

Multiplication

סוגריים
Sograyim

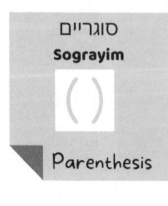

Parenthesis

אחוז
Achuz

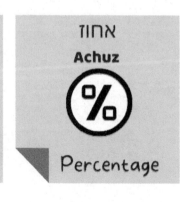

Percentage

אוניברסיטה
ONIVERSITA
UNIVERSITY

מפעל
MIF'AL
FACTORY

בניין
BINYAN
BUILDING

כלא
KELE
JAIL

בניין העיריה
BINYAN HA'IRIYA
TOWN HALL

גשר
GESHER
BRIDGE

טירה
TIRA
CASTLE

בית קברות
BEIT KVAROT
CEMETERY

מזרקה
MIZRAKA
FOUNTAIN

מנהרה
MINHARA
TUNNEL

גן חיות
GAN CHAYOT
ZOO

בית משפט
BEIT MISHPAT
COURT

קרקס
KIRKAS
CIRCUS

קזינו
KAZINO
CASINO

מעבדה
MA'ABADA
LABORATORY

חומרים

CHOMARIM

MATERIALS

כותנה
Kutna

Cotton

עץ
Etz

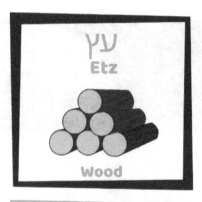

Wood

לבנה
Levena

Brick

בטון
Beton

Concrete

צמר
Tzemer

Wool

עור
Or

Leather

מתכת
Matechet

Metal

שיש
Shayish

Marble

פלדה
Plada

Steel

חרסינה
Charsina

Porcelain

חרס
Cheres

Clay

פלסטיק
Plastik

Plastic

גומי
Gumi

Rubber

נייר
Niyar

Paper

חול
Chol

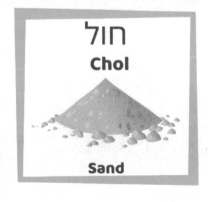

Sand

כדור הארץ
Kadur ha'aretz

Earth

רעידת אדמה re'idat adama earthquake	אש esh fire	שדה sade field
מפולת שלגים mapolet slagim avalanche	טורנדו tornado tornado	צוק tzuk cliff
אוקיינוס okyanus ocean	הר געש har ga'ash volcano	דיונה dyuna dune
גל gal wave	גבעה giv'a hill	קרחון kaechon glacier
ג'ונגל jungel jungle	עמק emek valley	מערה me'ara cave

תזמורת
TIZMORET
ORCHESTRA

שיר
SHIR
SONG

מוזיקאי
MUZIKA'I
MUSICIAN

גיטרה
GITARA
GUITAR

זמר
ZAMAR
SINGER

פסנתר
PSANTER
PIANO

תופים
TUPIM
DRUMS

כינור
KINOR
VIOLIN

חצוצרה
CHATZOTZRA
TRUMPET

מילים
MILIM
LYRICS

קהל
KAHAL
AUDIENCE

קול
KOL
VOICE

מיקרופון
MIKROFON
MICROPHONE

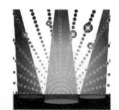

במה
BAMA
STAGE

עוצמה
OTZMA
VOLUME

כתובת
Ktovet
Address

מעטפה
Metafah
Envelope

תיבת דואר
Tevat doar
Mailbox

דואר
Doar
Mail

חותמת
Chotemet
Stamp

קבלה
Kabala
Bill

חשמל
Chashmal
Electricity

גז
Gaz
Gas

משכורת
Maskoret
Salary

מנוי
Manuy
Subscription

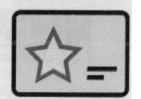

חבילה
Chavila
Package

דוור
Davar
Postman

לשלוח
Lishloach
Send

לקנות
Liknot
Buy

למכור
Limkor
Sell

אקולוגיה
ekologya

ecology

מחזור
MICHZUR
RECYCLE

סביבה
SVIVA
ENVIRONMENT

זיהום
ZIHUM
POLLUTION

חומרי הדברה
CHOMREY HADBARA
PESTICIDES

אורגני
ORGANI
ORGANIC

צמחוני
TZIMCHONI
VEGETARIAN

אנרגיה
ANERGYA
ENERGY

פחם
PECHAM
COAL

דלק
DELEK
GASOLINE

גרעיני
GAR'INI
NUCLEAR

מערכת אקולוגית
MA'ARECHET EKOLOGIT
ECOSYSTEM

עולם החי
OLAM HACHAY
FAUNA

צמחיה
TZIMCHIYA
FLORA

טמפרטורה
TEMPERATURA
TEMPERATURE

קוטב
KOTEV
ARCTIC

Made in the USA
Las Vegas, NV
18 November 2024

12077939R00044